SOMETHING AFTER NIGHT

AND OTHER POEMS

By

J. DANSON SMITH

Author of "100 Best Loved Poems" etc.

Published by
B. McCALL BARBOUR
28 George IV Bridge, Edinburgh EH1 1ES, Scotland

First Edition

(in this style)

1976

© B. McCall Barbour

Made and Printed in Great Britain by
Stanley L. Hunt (Printers) Ltd, Midland Road, Rushden, Northants

THROUGH CLOUD AND SUNSHINE

" I had fainted, unless I had believed to see the goodness of the Lord in the land of the living." Psa. xxvii. 13.

" In the daytime also He led them with a cloud, and all the night with a light of fire." Psa. lxxviii. 14.

" He led them on safely, so that they feared not." Psa. lxxviii. 33.

THROUGH " Cloud and Sunshine "—these comprise life's story,—
Those clouds which come, and curtain out our day ;
Not clouds of sin,—but burdens,—disappointments—
Unwanted and unwelcome things, which come our way.

And yet, these clouds may have a sunlit lining,—
For cloudless glory ever shines Above :
We do not well—by sighing or repining ;
'Tis better that we trust our Father's love.

Clouds have their use, else Nature would not have them ;
And shadow-making things enrich the soul :
Not always at the time is this apparent ;
It will be clearer when we reach life's goal.

But sunshine comes, as well as sombre shadows ;
And Time could mark full many a golden day
When purest joys our human hearts enraptured—
A foretaste given of bliss to last for aye.

And, at the last, when life its course hath ended,—
When Heaven is reached through Christ's redeeming grace,—
The clouds will all have passed,—and endless sunshine
Will be the constant bliss of that dear place.

REMEMBRANCE

" I will remember the years of the right hand of the most High." Psa. lxxvii. 10.

" Thou shalt remember all the way which the Lord thy God led thee." Deut. viii. 2.

" My soul shall be satisfied as with marrow and fatness ; and my mouth shall praise Thee with joyful lips : when I remember Thee upon my bed, and meditate on Thee in the night watches. Because Thou hast been my help, therefore in the shadow of Thy wings will I rejoice." Psa. lxiii. 5, 6, 7.

I WILL remember—'tis good to remember—
    Years that are past of God's goodness and grace ;
To brood once again over memories tender ;
    God's gracious dealings to grateful retrace.

Safely, indeed, hath His guiding hand led me,
    Through all life's highways and byways till now ;
Richly, indeed, hath His bounteous hand fed me,
    Even in famine,—though I knew not how.

Yea, in the sorrows which sometimes o'ertook me
    He was my succour, my strength and my stay :
And in calamities which sorely shook me
    He so supported, faith did not give way.

In such remembrance, reflection, recalling,
    Heart findeth confidence, mind grows serene ;
Shall not His right hand, which kept me from falling,
    Be still as strong as in past it hath been ?

SONGS IN THE NIGHT

" God my Maker, Who giveth songs in the night." Job. xxxv. 10.

" At midnight Paul and Silas prayed, and sang praises unto God : and the prisoners heard them." Acts xvi. 25.

THEIR backs were sore ; their feet were tied ;
'Twas midnight—sleep was quite denied ;
'Twas inky dark—they had no light ;
'Twas darker than the darkest night :
They could not view each other's face
In that foul, damp, and wretched place.

Their God, Whom they so truly served,
Had somehow not their lot preserved ;
Outraged, maltreated—did He care ?
Then why their state,—and why they there ?
But—dismal, doubting, dark dismay
They knew not—or else chased away.

They could not sleep ! They prayed ; they sang !
Their voices through the prison rang !
The prisoners from their sleep were stirred,—
Such sounds at midnight ne'er were heard ;
And God in heaven their song heard, too,
And instant shewed what He would do.

An earthquake—! How the strong place rocked !
How hardened hearts were quickly shocked !
How well-barred doors wide open swung,
And bolts and bars aside were flung :
And over all a sense of fear,—
A sense, perhaps, that God was near.

And work was done, and lives were blest ;
And Christ was openly confessed :
And souls were saved, were cleansed, forgiven ;
Made heirs of God, and heirs of heaven ;
While choirs above with praises rang,
Perchance—because God's brave men sang.

WHICH WINGS?

"And I said, Oh that I had wings like a dove! for then would I fly away, and be at rest. Lo, then would I wander far off, and remain in the wilderness. I would hasten my escape from the windy storm and tempest." Psa. lv. 6-8.

"Be merciful unto me, O God, be merciful unto me: for my soul trusteth in Thee: yea, in the shadow of Thy wings will I make my refuge, until these calamities be overpast." Psa. lvii. 1.

"Be merciful unto me, O God: for man would swallow me up; he fighting daily oppresseth me. . . . What time I am afraid, I will trust in Thee." Psa. lvi. 1, 3.

"Surely He shall deliver thee from the snare of the fowler, and from the noisome pestilence. He shall cover thee with his feathers, and under His wings shalt thou trust." Psa. xci. 3-4.

OH, for the wings of a dove! we sigh;
    From all our troubles and ills we would fly:
    We would fly away and would be at rest,
And deem that at last we were truly blest.

But the wings come not—though the sighs remain;
And the prayers and pleadings for wings are vain:
In the midst of trouble our lot may stay:
It would be our loss could we fly away.

There are wings—not those of the gentle dove—
Yea, wings of shelter, of strength and love;
Not wings wherewith we away may fly,
But wings—our refuge—as years pass by.

In the strong, safe shelter of those Great Wings
How safe are we from all evil things;
And there, safe guarded, can naught molest;
And in such hiding shall we have rest.

THEY STOOD STILL, LOOKING SAD

" Two of them went that same day to a village called Emmaus. . . . They talked together of all those things which had happened. . . . Jesus Himself drew near, and went with them . . . and said unto them ' What manner of communications are these that ye have one to another, as ye walk ? ' And they stood still, looking sad." Lu. xxiv. 13-17.

THEY stood still looking sad that day ;
Their hearts were filled with blank dismay ;
Their hopes were blighted—prospects dead :
Their golden dreams had quickly fled :
The One on Whom their hopes were set,
A felon's death had strangely met ;
And none could tell them, or explain
Why all they lived for now seemed vain.

Perchance, 'midst this world's war and woe,
We, too, some sudden shock may know :
The day-dreams, pondered o'er and o'er,
Alas, can be our dreams no more :
Some lightning-stroke has chased away
The dreams we cherished yesterday :
And sore and stricken, mute we brood,
In silence and in solitude.

But One " drew near " that shadowed day !
Their grief seemed strangely soothed away !
He still can come in grief's dark hour
With wondrous, soothing, healing power ;
Can reach the darkest depths we know
Of sorest sorrow, deepest woe :
His sympathy can bring relief
To what may be o'erwhelming grief.

THE BLESSINGS OF GOODNESS

" Thou preventest him with the blessings of goodness." Psa. xxi. 3.

" The earth is full of the goodness of the Lord." Psa. xxxiii. 5.

" The goodness of God endureth continually." Psa. lii. 1.

" Thou preparest a table before me in the presence of mine enemies : Thou anointest my head with oil ; my cup runneth over. Surely goodness and mercy shall follow me all the days of my life." Psa. xxiii. 5-6.

BLESSINGS of Goodness ! Ah, these come our way ;
These fill our cup on the dreariest day ;
Could we but see them we grateful would say—
  " Thanks for the blessings of goodness ! "

Plain is their form, and not showy their style ;
Neither to charm us, nor yet to beguile ;
But to support us through each stretching mile—
  Such are the blessings of goodness.

'Tis God Who gives them,—by Him are we blest ;
Food for the body, and peace for the breast :
Strength for our toils, and at evening time rest ;
  Such are the blessings of goodness.

For all the blessings which fill up our days
What shall we render ? say, what shall we raise ?
Surely a song of thanksgiving and praise
  Yea,—for the blessings of goodness.

HIS RIGHT HAND

"In the day of my trouble I sought the Lord; my sore ran in the night, and ceased not: my soul refused to be comforted." Psa. lxxvii. 2.

"Will the Lord cast off for ever, and will He be favourable no more?" Psa. lxxvii. 7.

"And I said, This is my infirmity; but I will remember the years of the right hand of the most High." Psa. lxxvii. 10.

WHERE shall I look when dark threat'ning clouds frighten?
  Where find my strength when molested by fears?
When mists hang low, and no prospect doth brighten,—
  Where shall I look,—save again at past years?

Years in which oft darkly veiled was the morrow:
  Years when the outlook was gloomy and grim:
Years when the cup sometimes o'erflowed with sorrow;
  When life was hopeless, indeed, but for Him.

Yet, years in which His hand truly protected;
  Years when we found Him unfailing and true:
Years when all safe through life's maze He directed,
  Opening paths which were unto us new.

Still His right hand unto us is extended,—
  Hand of our God,—to protect and provide;
Hand that will lead until life here is ended;
  In that good Hand we can safely confide.

POSTPONED BLESSINGS

" The Lord blessed the latter end of Job more than his beginning." Job xlii. 12.

" They have no wine . . . Jesus saith unto them, Fill the waterpots with water. And they filled them up to the brim. And He saith unto them, Draw out now . . . When the ruler of the feast had tasted the water that was made wine . . . the governor of the feast called the bridegroom and saith . . . Thou hast kept the good wine until now." Jno. ii. 3-10.

" There failed not ought of any good thing which the Lord had spoken unto the house of Israel ; all came to pass." Josh. xxi. 45.

" I had fainted, unless I had believed to see the goodness of the Lord in the land of the living." Psa. xxvii. 13.

WE deem them as denied us—things which come not our way,
Things we so much have wanted, for which we, urgent, pray ;
We cannot tell the reason, the answer is not given ;
Nor why the things so wanted are granted not from heaven.

We reason and we question,—conjecture and conclude ;
We come to rash assumptions, which ne'er can do us good ;
We deem God hath denied us : resigned, we mutely sigh,—
Indulge in morbid broodings as months or years go by.

But things which seemed denied us withheld may only be
Till times for their enjoyment reach suitability ;
Postponed—to yet be granted,—withheld to yet be given,
Are multitudes of blessings to reach us yet from heaven.

NOT NOW, BUT AFTERWARDS

"What I do thou knowest not now; but thou shalt understand hereafter." John xiii. 7. (R.V.)

"Whither I go, thou canst not follow Me now; but thou shalt follow Me afterwards." John xiii. 36.

"Eye hath not seen, nor ear heard, neither have entered into the heart of man, the things which God hath prepared for them that love Him." 1 Cor. ii. 8.

NOT now, but afterwards, when safe in glory,
   We'll read the meaning of life's chequered years ;
We'll understand completely then life's story ;
   We'll know the value of its grief and tears.

Not now, but afterwards, things now perplexing,—
   The mysteries, perhaps, of life-long pain,
The dark enigmas, and the things sore vexing,
   In heaven's strong flood-light will be clear and plain.

Not now, but afterwards, with undimmed vision,
   We'll see that God was working all for good ;
Our loss down here, and every hard decision,
   Will then, at last, be fully understood.

Not now, but afterwards, we'll share the rapture—
   His welcome home—and mayhap His embrace :
Oh, joy of joys, if we shall then but capture
   One glimpse which tells we pleased Him in life's race.

UNSOUNDED WELLS

"They came to Elim, where were twelve wells of water, and threescore and ten palm trees : and they encamped there by the waters." Ex. xv. 27.

"Behold, God is my salvation ; I will trust, and not be afraid : for the Lord Jehovah is my strength and my song ; He also is become my salvation. Therefore with joy shall ye draw water out of the wells of salvation." Is. xii. 2-3.

"Jacob's well was there. Jesus therefore, being wearied with His journey, sat thus on the well." Jno. iv. 6.

WE have read of the wells of salvation :
    God's wells—why, of course, they must be ;
The wells where the jaded and weary
    From languor and thirst are set free.

No pilgrim their depth hath e'er sounded ;
    Exhaustless their wealth doth remain :
Upspringing ; refreshing ; life-giving ;
    None e'er from these wells draw in vain.

Unfailing these wells of salvation ;
    Abiding and full their supply :
No fear need assail any pilgrim
    That these wells shall ever run dry.

My soul, at these wells of salvation
    Drink often ; drink deeply ; drink long :
The road and the load, howe'er taxing,
    Shall find thee unjaded and strong.

THEY SANG AN HYMN

" Jesus said unto them, this is My blood of the covenant, which is shed for many. Verily I say unto you, I will no more drink of the fruit of the vine, until that day when I drink it new in the Kingdom of God. And when they had sung an hymn, they went out unto the Mount of Olives." Mar. xiv. 24/26. (R.V.)

" At midnight Paul and Silas prayed, and sang praises unto God."—Acts xvi. 25.

'TWAS night indeed ; their darkest night ;
 They deemed it their last night with Him :
 Yet, ere they left the chamber bright,
We read that they all sang an hymn.

Their hearts were sad ; they would be left :
 He Whom they loved would soon be gone :
And they, benighted and bereft,
 Would have Him not—to lean upon.

And yet they sang, with voices brave,
 And strengthened each his brother-friend :
Their sky was dark, the issue grave ;
 Their future none could comprehend.

They sang : and if some eyes were dim,—
 If choking sense nigh stilled the song,
Perchance they may have strengthened Him,—
 So soon to meet the rabble throng.

" They sang "—thus speaks the record true :
 " They sang an hymn " that darkest night !
And, soul of mine, do thou sing, too,
 Should tragic mysteries steal thy light.

STILL WITH THEE

"How precious also are Thy thoughts unto me, O God! how great is the sum of them! If I should count them, they are more in number than the sand: when I awake, I am still with Thee." Psa. cxxxix. 17-18.

"When my spirit was overwhelmed within me, then Thou knewest my path." Psa. cxlii. 3.

"If I take the wings of the morning, and dwell in the uttermost parts of the sea; even there shall Thy hand lead me, and Thy right hand shall hold me." Psa. cxxxix. 9-10.

"He shall call upon Me, and I will answer him: I will be with him in trouble; I will deliver him, and honour him." Psa. xci. 15.

STILL, still with Thee, through all life's passing changes!
   Still, still with Thee, through all its fleeting years!
Still, still with Thee, though undesired exchanges
   Have tried the heart, it may be—drawn the tears.

Still, still with Thee, in joy as well as sorrow;
   Still, still with Thee, in weakness and in health:
Still, still with Thee, e'en with life's veiled to-morrow;
   Still, still with Thee in want as well as wealth.

Still, still with Thee! Some dear ones, fondly cherished,
   Have passed beyond—are now within the veil:
Still, still with Thee, though one-time joys have perished,
   And lights which cheered, alas, have now grown pale.

Still, still with Thee, in quiet, safe abiding!
   Still, still with Thee, and therefore knowing rest;
Still, still with Thee in calm and sweet confiding;
   Still, still with Thee—and thus supremely blest.

WHY GO I MOURNING?

"I mourn in my complaint . . . because of the voice of the enemy." Psa. lv. 2/3.

"Why go I mourning because of the oppression of the enemy. . . . Hope thou in God: for I shall yet praise Him, Who is the health of my countenance, and my God." Psa. xlii. 9/11.

"Yea, in the shadow of Thy wings will I make my refuge, until these calamities be overpast. . . . I will cry unto God. . . . I will sing and give praise." Psa. lvii. 1, 2, 7.

WHY go I mourning, why go I mourning,—
   Mourning because of the enemy's voice?
Why doth my soul seem poured out within me?
   Should not a child of the Highest rejoice?

God hath forgotten me—thus it now seemeth;
   "Where is thy God?" is the oft-taunting sneer:
Why doth He stay His strong hand of deliverance—
   If He regardeth me; if He doth hear?

Tears, bitter tears, day and night form my portion:
   Cast down my soul,—and disquiet within:
Deep calls to deep, as the billows sweep over me,
   Darkness, oppression, but no sense of sin.

What shall I do 'midst the dark and oppression?
   Where shall I go 'midst the fury and strife?
Singing shall conquer Satanic depression,—
   Singing to God, yea, the God of my life.

Sing then, my soul, of past mercy and goodness;
   Sing because God, thy God, cannot forget:
Sing because God will command loving-kindness;
   Sing,—sing in faith,—thou shalt sure praise Him yet.

WORKING TOGETHER

" We know that all things work together for good to them that love God, to them who are the called according to His purpose." Rom. viii. 28.

" Joseph said unto them, Fear not : for am I in the place of God ? But as for you, ye thought evil against me ; but God meant it unto good, to bring to pass, as it is this day, to save much people alive." Gen. 1. 19-20.

" It is good for me that I have been afflicted ; that I might learn Thy statutes. Before I was afflicted I went astray: but now have I kept Thy word." Psa. cxix. 71, 67.

WORKING together—the good and the bad ;
Working together—the bright and the sad ;
Working together—both comfort and pain ;
Working together—for good we may gain.

Working together—the pleasant and ill ;
Working together—the rough seas and still ;
Things which are clear with things not understood;
Working together—and all for our good.

Working together—both sorrow and joy ;
Things which delight, and things which annoy ;
Things which are welcome, and things which are odd,
Working for good unto them that love God.

Working together ! And how is it done ?
Ah, 'tis the work of the Wonderful One :
If we but love Him, then things smooth or rude
All work together for our certain good.

THE UNWANTED

" He is despised and rejected of men; a Man of sorrows, and acquainted with grief." Is. liii. 3.

" Reproach hath broken My heart; and I am full of heaviness: and I looked for some to take pity, but there was none; and for comforters, but I found none." Psa. lxix. 20.

" Mine own familiar friend . . . hath lifted up his heel against me." Psa. xli. 9.

" Come unto Me, all ye that labour and are heavy laden, and I will give you rest." Mat. xi. 28.

" There is a Friend that sticketh closer than a brother." Pro. xviii. 24.

WHERE shall I go when my heart is sore,
   And I feel unwanted and lone?
When those who loved me—now love no more;
   When joys of the past have flown?

Unwanted! Unwanted! The sad word sounds;
   And I know to my cost 'tis true:
Unwanted! Unwanted! The word resounds,—
   It echoes my being through.

Unwanted! And thus, as I feel forlorn,
   Shall I yearn for my journey's end?
Shall my sad heart wish I had ne'er been born?
   Shall I say I have not a friend?

There's a Friend for the friendless—a Friend divine,—
   He ever wants me I know;
His love reaches down to these depths of mine,
   So unto this Friend I'll go.

THINGS WE KNOW

"These things have I written unto you that believe on the name of the Son of God ; that ye may know that ye have eternal life." 1 Jno. v. 13.

"We know that we have passed from death unto life, because we love the brethren." 1 Jno iii. 14.

"Beloved, now are we the sons of God, and it doth not yet appear what we shall be : but we know that, when He shall appear, we shall be like Him ; for we shall see Him as He is." 1 Jno. iii. 2.

"We know that all things work together for good to them that love God, to them who are the called according to His purpose." Rom. viii. 28.

HOW blest to know our sins are all forgiven !
    That on that bright, that glad, eternal Day
  No spot, or stain, or shadowed thing shall linger,
For Christ's own blood hath washed them all away.

How good to know, as meanwhile here we journey,
    That dark enigmas,—things not understood,—
Things causing pain and heartache, grief and travail,—
    That all these things shall yet work for our good.

How sweet to know that yonder in the Glory,
    Beyond this scene of sorrow, sin and strife,
The Father's House awaits, with many mansions,—
    The peerless home for our unending life.

How grand to know that He Himself is coming !
    He said He'd come ! He may not long delay !
And any hour, yea, in an eyelid's twinkling,
    Our joy may be—we have been caught away.

THEIR NET BRAKE

" Master . . . at Thy word I will let down the net. And when they had this done, they inclosed a great multitude of fishes : and their net brake. And they beckoned unto their partners, which were in the other ship, that they should come and help them. And they came, and filled both the ships, so that they began to sink." Lu. v. 5/7.

" Jesus said unto Simon, Fear not ; from henceforth thou shalt catch men."—Lu. v. 10.

" Seek ye first the Kingdom of God, and His righteousness ; and all these things shall be added unto you."—Mat. vi. 33.

THEIR net—it brake ! They would not need it more ;
   'Twas filled with fishes—more than they could think ;
They filled two ships, and hastened for the shore,
   And, lo, the ships themselves began to sink.

Their net—it brake ! Strange circumstance indeed !
   The Master-Fisher's work had made the rent !
Henceforth, not fish—but men, they were to heed
   Was, clear, the lesson which the Master meant.

For some,—doth break the net of human skill ;
   No longer " fishing " is to be life's aim :
Before them lies a new but clear-cut Will :
   Upon them falls a new but Sovereign claim.

Fear not, O soul, if He is calling thee
   Boats, nets, and things familiar now to leave ;
Fear not,—shrink not,—thine eyes are yet to see
   Far greater things than thou canst now perceive.

And of the needs,—the human needs,—just this—
   When nets, much used, have broken in His Will,
He then shall meet all needs,—that care is His,—
   And thine shall be to watch His Sovereign skill.

GOD-GIVEN GOODNESSES

" Having food and raiment let us be therewith content."
1 Tim. vi. 8.

" Let Thy saints rejoice in goodness." II Chr. vi. 41.

" The living God, Who giveth us richly all things to enjoy."
I Tim. vi. 17.

" Blessed be the Lord, Who daily loadeth us with benefits, even the God of our salvation." Psa. lxviii. 19.

WITH pleasure now I pen this little message !
 I cannot greet you, yet would make you glad
In musing on the blessings and the bounties,—
The God-giv'n goodnesses which we have had.

The common things—at least we deem them common—
 The daily bread,—the strength for each day's task,—
The wondrous health,—the fitness for the journey,
 With these—what more of earth's things need we ask ?

And hallowed things—the joy of sacred union,—
 Of love,—and loves,—blest ties upon life's road ;
Of friendships, too, and precious sweet communion:—
 These, these are all the priceless gifts of God.

And Heavenly things,—the joy of sins forgiven ;
 And God's dear Book, to bless us day by day ;
And with us, too, the Comforter from Heaven,
 To bear us on the upward, heavenly way.

REJOICING

" Philip . . . preached unto him Jesus . . . and he baptized him. And when they were come up out of the water, the Spirit of the Lord caught away Philip, that the eunuch saw him no more : and he went on his way rejoicing." Acts viii. 35/40.

" The disciples were filled with joy, and with the Holy Ghost." Acts. xiii. 52.

" Let all those that put their trust in Thee rejoice ; let them ever shout for joy . . . let them also that love Thy name be joyful in Thee." Psa. v. 11.

" I will rejoice in the Lord, I will joy in the God of my salvation." Hab. iii. 18.

HE went on his way rejoicing,—
   Rejoicing in light from heaven ;
   Rejoicing in peace and pardon ;
Rejoicing in sins forgiven.

He went on his way rejoicing,
   Alone, yet with soul so light !
His joy in a new-found Saviour
   Made everything now so bright.

He went on his way rejoicing !
   'Twas pardon, and peace, and rest !
A full and a free salvation !
   How richly he now was blest !

And when the long journey ended,
   And ties were renewed again,
The joy of his new salvation
   Would speak to his fellow-men.

UNWANING TREASURE

" I am the Lord, I change not." Mal. iii. 6.

" Can a woman forget her sucking child, that she should not have compassion on the son of her womb ? yea, they may forget, yet will I not forget thee." Isa. xlix. 15.

" God my exceeding joy." Psa. xliii. 4.

" Jesus Christ the same yesterday, and to-day, and for ever." Heb. xiii. 8.

MIDST all the things which change and pass and perish,—
    The blessings which so oft seem growing dim,—
How good it is to calmly, truly cherish
    The treasure which is ours in having Him.

His love unchanged throughout the years abideth,
    When other loves have changed or passed away ;
No aching, breaking heart in Him confideth
    But finds its night of sorrow turned to day.

His care,—His wondrous care, is wrapped around us;
    Nor grows He weary though we oft-times fall :
His mercies, like His mercy, they surround us ;
    He bends a listening ear whene'er we call.

Ah, yes, we have in Him unwaning treasure,—
    Forgiveness, love, compassion, matchless grace ;
May it be ours to give Him back some pleasure,
    As daily in His will our steps we trace.

TWELVE HOURS IN THE DAY

"Jesus saith, Let us go into Judæa again. His disciples say unto Him, Master, the Jews of late sought to stone Thee; and goest Thou thither again? Jesus answered, Are there not twelve hours in the day?" John xi. 4/10.

"In nothing be anxious, but in everything by prayer and supplication with thanksgiving let your requests be made known unto God." Phil. iv. 6. (R.V.)

"Trust in the Lord with all thine heart, and lean not unto thine own understanding: in all thy ways acknowledge Him, and He shall direct thy paths." Prov. iii. 5/6.

"ARE there not twelve hours in the day?" He said,
   As calmly He took His way!
He feared no evil, He knew no dread,
   Nor terror, nor dark dismay.

Unrushed, unhurried, His work was done;
   No worker so wise as He:
From early morning till setting sun
   He laboured unceasingly.

"Are there not twelve hours in the day?" we ask—
   When the calls and the claims would make
A fever instead of a well done task.
   Shall we not to His words betake?

"Twelve hours, twelve hours in the day," we'll say,
   When by a thousand claims pressed;
And fears and fevers will steal away;
   And we'll know His keeping and rest.

CALM ASSURANCE

" Great peace have they which love Thy law : and nothing shall offend them." Psa. cxix. 165.

" My people shall dwell in a peaceable habitation, and in sure dwellings, and in quiet resting places, when it shall hail, coming down on the forest." Is. xxxii. 18-19.

" Thou wilt keep him in perfect peace, whose mind is stayed on Thee : because he trusteth in Thee." Is. xxvi. 3.

" Be careful for nothing ; but in every thing by prayer and supplication, with thanksgiving, let your requests be made known unto God. And the peace of God, which passeth all understanding, shall keep your hearts and minds through Christ Jesus." Phil. iv. 6-7.

GREAT peace have they, and quiet, calm assurance,
    Who love God's law, and on it daily feed ;
They have a strength, a power and an endurance,
    Which strangely nerves them in the hour of need.

Deep peace have they whose whole imagination,
    Whose mind and thought on God are constant stayed ;
How free they are from fevered agitation,
    And nothing seems to make their soul afraid.

God's peace it is,—which passeth understanding,—
    Keeps heart and mind where lives are lived in prayer ;
And troubles which confront, howe'er commanding,
    Drive not the soul thus kept to dire despair.

And so—in troubled days may this assurance,
    This calm assurance, keep your heart and mine ;
We need no power of special, strong endurance,
    Enough—His peace,—His wondrous peace divine.

HE OFT REFRESHED ME

"The Lord give mercy unto the house of Onesiphorus; for he oft refreshed me and was not ashamed of my chain. But when he was in Rome he sought me out very diligently and found me. . . . In how many things he ministered unto me at Ephesus, thou knowest very well." 2 Tim. i. 16/18.

"I am glad of the coming of Stephanas and Fortunatus and Achaicus; for that which was lacking on your part they have supplied. For they have refreshed my spirit." 2 Cor. xvi. 17/18.

"HE oft refreshed me!" Tribute truly rare;
"At Ephesus He showed much human care:
   At Rome He sought me out,—true friend, indeed,—
My 'chain' disturbed Him not—since I had need."

Yes, tribute rare! Yet, what a service given!
How great the value placed on it in heaven!
Just to have braced and blest that warrior true—!
Angels could well have wished that work to do.

"He oft refreshed me!" Well, when we have run
Life's earthly race,—when service here is done,—
Will our earned tribute, fadeless, lasting, be—
"He oft refreshed, and oft-times strengthened me"?

Words, acts, devotion,—time for thoughtful care,
Life in the spirit,—fellowship in prayer,—
Selfless absorption—not in cares my own,—
These earn that tribute, these, and these alone.

UNCEASING GOODNESS

"The Lord hath prepared His throne in the heavens; and His kingdom ruleth over all." Psa. ciii. 19.

"Surely goodness and mercy shall follow me all the days of my life." Psa. xxiii. 6.

"He left not Himself without witness, in that He did good, and gave us rain from heaven, and fruitful seasons, filling our hearts with food and gladness." Acts xiv. 17.

"Seek ye first the kingdom of God, and His righteousness; and all these things shall be added unto you." Matt. vi. 33.

CLOUDS drape the world; for God hath been neglected;
    And unleashed evil forces seem to win!
The Arch Destroyer's work may be detected,
    For everywhere there stalks unbridled sin.

But God abides! His goodness is unceasing!
    His sun still shines! His rain it still doth fall!
The earth its fruits is constantly releasing!
    He hears and answers all who on Him call!

Unceasing goodness! Yea, 'midst all life's sorrow,—
    'Midst all earth's travail, tragedy and woe;
With all its dark, and so uncertain morrow,—
    We may unceasing goodness from Him know.

The flowers still bloom; the trees wear their adorning;
    The little birds, untroubled, sweetly sing;
And we, His own, yea, children of the Morning,
    Look for the day when Christ shall reign as King.

WORKING WHILE WITH THEM

"There was at Joppa a certain disciple named Tabitha; which by interpretation is called Dorcas: this woman was full of good works and alms deeds which she did. And it came to pass in those days, that she was sick and died. . . . They laid her in an upper chamber. . . . When Peter was come, they brought him into the upper chamber: and all the widows stood by him weeping, and shewing the coats and garments which Dorcas made while she was with them." Acts ix. 37/39.

"As we have therefore opportunity, let us do good unto all men, especially unto them who are of the household of faith." Gal. vi. 10.

HER hands were truly nimble,
   She worked with holy joy,—
With scissors, needle, thimble
She did the hours employ.
With purpose and with passion
   She coats and garments made,—
Conformed to worthy fashion,
   Though she for none was paid.

She worked while she was with them,
   And, when she fell asleep,
The widows gathered round her
   To mourn, lament, and weep.
With good deeds, and with alms-deeds,
   Her life had held rich store,
But now her hands were folded,
   And she would toil no more.

"She worked while she was with them!"
   That time alone is ours
For ministry and service,
   With all life's wondrous powers.
If we would work for others
   We must not brook delay,
But work "while we are with them",—
   And thus begin to-day.

UNDYING LOVE

"Having loved His own which were in the world, He loved them unto the end" (the uttermost). Jno. xiii. 1.

"Yea, I have loved thee with an everlasting love : therefore with lovingkindness have I drawn thee." Jer. xxxi. 3.

"Love is strong as death. . . . Many waters cannot quench love, neither can the floods drown it." Cant. viii. 6-7.

"Who shall separate us from the love of Christ?" Rom. viii. 35.

UNDYING love—'midst all that here doth perish !
    Undying love around us every day !
  'Midst all the loss of much our hearts did cherish—
    Undying love, attending, all the way.

Undying love ! Oh, wondrous, wondrous story !
    God was in Christ, Who gave Himself for me :
Undying love ! God sent Him from the glory
    To pay sin's debt, to die and set men free.

Thus what to-day be ours of joy or sorrow,
    Whate'er awaits us here, obscure or dim :
However dark may seem to us life's morrow,
    Undying love is ours, if we have Him.

And so, undying love shall aye attend us,
    Whate'er may fade or fail or pass away ;
Shall comfort, keep, provide, protect, defend us
    Until we reach Love's Home—Love's Perfect Day.

WHAT IS GOD LIKE?

"Philip saith unto Him (Jesus), Lord, shew us the Father, and it sufficeth us. Jesus saith unto him, Have I been so long time with you, and yet hast thou not known Me, Philip? He that hath seen Me hath seen the Father." John xiv. 8/9.

"No man hath seen God at any time; the only begotten Son, which is in the bosom of the Father, He hath declared Him." Jno. i. 18.

"God . . . hath in these last days spoken unto us by His Son . . . the express image of His person." Heb. i. 1/3.

"WHAT like is God?" 'Twas Philip's quest!
It grew and grew, and on him pressed;
To just see God, with eyes of sense,
Would be a wondrous recompense.

"What like is God?" The answer came—
"Thou seest Me—I am the same;
Who seeth Me—the Father sees,"
Words meant to Philip's quest appease.

"What like is God?" We ask it still
With finite mind, with restless will;
Still make the same beseeching cry—
"Lord, shew . . . our longing satisfy."

Have we seen Jesus,—wondrous, fair;
His grace and love beyond compare;
In His blest company have been?
Then, we the Father, too, have seen.

UNREMITTING CARE

" Casting all your care upon Him : for He careth for you."
I Pet. v. 7.

" Jesus was in the hinder part of the ship, asleep on a pillow : and they awake Him, and say unto Him, Master carest Thou not that we perish ? And He arose, and rebuked the wind, and said unto the sea, Peace, be still." Mark iv. 38-39.

" The hireling fleeth, because he is an hireling, and careth not for the sheep. I am the Good Shepherd, and know My sheep, and am known of Mine. As the Father knoweth Me, even so know I the Father : and I lay down My life for the sheep." Jno. x. 13-15.

" O fear the Lord, ye His saints : for there is no want to them that fear Him. The young lions do lack and suffer hunger : but they that seek the Lord shall not want any good thing." Psa. xxxiv. 9-10.

THE strain of life more testing grows ;
    More taxing now the things which wear ;
But heart and mind have for repose—
    God's unremitting care.

Life's problems grow ; its limits press ;
    More now abundant—things to bear :
Yet, peace can reign in all distress,
    Through unremitting care.

The shadows deepen ; evils reign :
    And sorrow's cup full many share :
Yet hearts find comfort, 'midst life's pain,
    In unremitting care.

Our God still reigns ! His hand controls !
    And nothing can His love outwear :
And we, who trust to Him our souls,
    Find unremitting care.

CHRIST AT THE TABLE

" Two of them went that same day to a village called Emmaus . . . and while they communed together and reasoned, Jesus Himself drew near, and went with them. . . . They constrained Him, saying Abide with us : for it is toward evening, and the day is far spent. And He went in to tarry with them. And . . . as He sat at meat with them, He took bread, and blest it, and brake, and gave to them." Lu. xxiv. 13/31.

" As soon then as they were come to land, they saw a fire of coals there, and fish laid thereon, and bread. . . . Jesus saith unto them, Come and dine." Jno. xxi. 5/10.

" HE sat—at meat—with them,—"
This Stranger of the day ;
His wondrous talk had blest their souls
Along the dusty way.

" He sat—at meat—with them ! "
Sat round the simple board !
This charming One, Whose words had warmed :
Unseen, unknown as Lord.

" He sat—at meat—with them ! "
He blest it, and He brake :
Their eyes were opened ! He was gone !
Then—how of Him they spake !

We, too, may thus be blest,
If at our board He shares :
Invited, welcomed, honoured Guest,—
Rich then most frugal fares !

THREEFOLD BLESSINGS

(Care, Love and Power)

" Trust in the Lord, and do good ; so shalt thou dwell in the land, and verily thou shalt be fed. . . . Commit thy way unto the Lord ; trust also in Him, and He shall bring it to pass." Psa. xxxvii. 3, 5.

" We have known and believed the love that God hath to us. God is love ; and he that dwelleth in love dwelleth in God, and God in him. . . . There is no fear in love ; but perfect love casteth out fear." I Jno. iv. 16, 18.

" He that loveth Me shall be loved of My Father, and I will love him, and will manifest Myself to him." Jno. xiv. 21.

" Almighty. . . . Therefore trust thou in Him." Job xxxv. 13-14.

WE all need **care** ! We want it, and we like it ;
    The happy sense that " someone cares for me " ;
And happier still if **love** to care is wedded :
    And then—if **power** is there—how wonderful these three !

Well, **He** doth care ; minutely ; greatly ; grandly :
    His care exceeds the fondest mother's art :
Since we are His then we shall find, most surely,
    To care for us, at all times, is His part.

And then—He **loves** ; how much—we cannot fathom :
    We are more dear to Him than angels fair ;
Those heavenly hosts enjoy unclouded glory :
    But we may know our Father's love and care.

Then He has **power** ; for, is He not almighty ?
    And naught there is that e'er can stay His hand :
Thus care, and love and power, for us united,
    Are more than all our needs shall e'er demand.

HEREAFTER !

"What I do thou knowest not now; but thou shalt know (understand) hereafter." Jno. xiii. 7.

"Praying always with all prayer and supplication in the Spirit, and watching thereunto with all perseverance. . . ." Eph. vi. 18.

"When John (Baptist) had heard in the prison the works of Christ, he sent two of his disciples, and said unto Him, Art Thou He that should come, or do we look for another? Jesus answered and said unto them, Go and shew John again those things which ye do hear and see. . . . And blessed is he, whosoever shall not be offended in Me." Mat. xi. 1/6.

HEREAFTER ! When? Ah, that we cannot know,—
    When things desired may unto us be given;
Perhaps they shall be ours yet, here below;
    Perhaps they shall not be till we reach heaven.

Hereafter ! When? Well, if 'tis not to-day
    Those asked-for things we felt were in His will
Come not to bless us, nor to cheer our way,
    Hereafter those requests He will fulfil.

Hereafter—? When shall we full understand
    The painful things, which nigh our hearts did break?
Perhaps down here; if not, in Heaven's clear land,
    When, in His likeness, we shall There awake.

Hereafter ! Word so full of wondrous scope !
    It takes all life in here,—then reaches on :
It fills the heart with restful, trustful hope,—
    A pillow which God's child can lean upon.

UNSWERVING FAITHFULNESS

"He is faithful that promised." Heb. x. 23.

"God is faithful, by whom ye were called unto the fellowship of His Son Jesus Christ our Lord." I Cor. i. 9.

"Faithful is He that calleth you." I Thes. v. 24.

"He abideth faithful : He cannot deny Himself." II Tim. ii. 13.

MIDST all life's fleeting changes,
    The things which fade and fail :
  The lights which once so gladdened
    But now grow dim and pale ;
It comforts and it heartens,
    Whate'er may pass away,
To know that He is faithful ;
    To find that He doth stay.

Sometimes He has to test us
    If He would faithful be ;
And then His acts we challenge ;
    The **end** we do not see :
But He abideth faithful ;
    And so, throughout each test,
He heeds not our complainings,
    But waits till we are blest.

So, through all lights and shadows,
    Through all life's nights and days,
Through all its varied problems,
    Through all its untried ways,
Unswerving, He'll be faithful,
    Will fail not nor forsake,
Will guide and guard and keep us,
    Till in Heaven's light we wake.

GOD IS WITH YOU

"He hath said, I will never leave thee, nor forsake thee, so that we may boldly say, The Lord is my helper . . ." Heb. xiii. 5/6.

"The angel of the Lord appeared unto him, and said unto him, The Lord is with thee, thou mighty man of valour." Jud. vi. 12.

"There stood by me this night the angel of God, whose I am, and whom I serve, saying, Fear not . . ." Acts xxvii. 23/24.

"GOD is with you!" So we've heard;
"God is with you!" Wondrous word!
Can ye lack, or need ye fear,
Having God Himself thus near?

"God is with you"—known by faith;
"With you" even as He saith:
Feelings fail—but facts abide,—
"God is with you,"—by your side!

God—all-sovereign,—with you now!
Foes and forces to Him bow!
Bold dictators rise and fall;
But God's Kingdom rules o'er all.

"God is with you!" Mind hath peace:
Heart,—from anxious fears, release:
Dread and tumult—all are gone,—
When this word we lean upon.

UNFATHOMED WEALTH

" Blessed be the God and Father of our Lord Jesus Christ, Who hath blessed us with all spiritual blessings. . . . Having predestinated us unto the adoption of children by Jesus Christ to Himself. . . . To the praise of the glory of His grace, wherein He hath made us accepted in the beloved." Eph. i. 3, 5, 6.

" That Christ may dwell in your hearts by faith ; that ye, being rooted and grounded in love, may be able to comprehend with all saints what is the breadth, and length, and depth, and height ; and to know the love of Christ, which passeth knowledge." Eph. iii. 17-19.

" Now unto Him that is able to do exceeding abundantly above all that we ask or think, according to the power that worketh in us, unto Him be glory." Eph. iii. 20-21.

" I will dwell in them, and walk in them ; and I will be their God, and they shall be My people. . . . I will be a Father unto you, and ye shall be my sons and daughters, saith the Lord Almighty." II Cor. vi. 16-18.

WE sigh for blessings past and gone ;
    For treasured joys, now passed away:
We find them meat to muse upon,
And wish them back, to with us stay.

Yet some can come not e'er again,
    However long the course of years ;
The conscious fact doth bring us pain ;
    The forceful truth may bring us tears.

But we are His ! Unfathomed wealth
    Is wrapped in this blest truth sublime !
Whate'er has gone—joys, riches, health—
    We are His own,—and for all time.

Unfathomed wealth ! Gold ne'er to dim !
    Supplies to flow while life shall last !
The wondrous wealth of having Him
    Is ours to know till time be past.

A LITTLE BOY'S LUNCH

" Whence shall we buy bread, that these may eat? . . . There is a lad here which hath five barley loaves and two small fishes; but what are they among so many? . . . Jesus said, Make the men sit down . . . When He had given thanks, He distributed to the disciples, and the disciples to them that were set down." Jno. vi. 5/14.

" His name shall be called Wonderful . . ." Isa. ix. 6.

" They were sore amazed in themselves beyond measure, and wondered. For they considered not the miracle of the loaves." Mark vi. 51/52.

FIVE little loaves, two fishes small,
A laddie's lunch, yea, that was all;
   But unto Him these things were given,
And, lifting up His eyes to Heaven,
These simple things He blest and brake,
And near ten thousand did partake.

Great sight indeed,—to sit and see
Those biscuits grow! Great mystery!
In His or His disciples' hands,
Obedient to unheard commands,
Those biscuits grew, and grew, and grew,—
Yet how,—none but the Saviour knew.

They all were fed—well fed indeed!
The hungriest got all he could need:
And lo, when they could eat no more
Twelve baskets full were still in store:
And some, perchance, received a share,
And homeward bore the wondrous fare.

" Great miracle "—we quickly say;
" The Saviour did His power display."
But " Wonderful " is still His name;
His power is still the very same:
And if my needs require such skill,
He'll work for me! He will! He will!

ILLIMITABLE RESOURCES

" Jesus saith, Whence shall we buy bread, that these may eat ? And this He said to prove him : for He Himself knew what He would do." Jno. vi. 5-6.

" Go thou to the sea, and cast an hook, and take up the fish that first cometh up ; and when thou hast opened his mouth, thou shalt find a piece of money : that take, and give unto them, for Me and thee." Mat. xvii. 27.

" I have not a cake, but an handful of meal in a barrel, and a little oil in a cruse. . . . The barrel of meal shall not waste, neither shall the cruse of oil fail, until the day that the Lord sendeth rain upon the earth. . . . And the barrel of meal wasted not, neither did the cruse of oil fail." I Kings xvii. 12, 14, 16.

" Although the fig tree shall not blossom, neither shall fruit be in the vines ; the labour of the olive shall fail, and the fields shall yield no meat ; the flock shall be cut off from the fold, and there shall be no herd in the stalls : yet I will rejoice in the Lord, I will joy in the God of my salvation." Hab. iii. 17-18.

OUR cruse of oil might well run dry.
    And time our barrel make quite bare :
    But these fail not ! The reason why— ?
We are our Father's care.

Perplexities sore on us press :
    We are shut in, with no way through :
No need for fear, alarm, distress—
    He knows what He will do.

Griefs come—like some o'erwhelming wave :
    They threaten to engulf and drown :
But He is there—still strong to save :
    And we shall not go down.

Thus through the days, the months, the years,
    His great resources we shall find ;
And we shall be immune from fears,
    With peace for heart and mind.

THE ELDER PRODIGAL

"Now his elder son was in the field; and as he came and drew nigh to the house, he heard musick and dancing . . . and he was angry, and would not go in." Lu. xv. 25/32.

"Walk worthy of the vocation wherewith ye are called, with all lowliness and meekness, with longsuffering, forbearing one another in love." Eph. iv. 1/3.

"Let nothing be done through strife or vainglory; but in lowliness of mind let each esteem other better than themselves." Phil. ii. 3, 4.

HE heard the music and the dance !
He understood it all, perchance;
Yet, stubbornness quite won the day,
No pleasant thing his tongue could say:
His long-lost brother—now returned,—
He welcomed not, but basely spurned:
While jealousy so filled his mind
That to all goodness he was blind.

His brother's error loomed full great,
While he had been immaculate !
To give him welcome, make a feast,
To kill the calf,—'twere not the least
Like what true justice should demand;
No, no, the feast by him was banned:
His father—he most truly erred—
His royal welcome was absurd !

* * * * *

Poor shrivelled soul ! Thy heart—how base;
How far removed from matchless grace:
Self-satisfied and smug withal,
Thy shrunken heart become so small !
God pity thee,—and all thy kind,
Who to the nobler things are blind—
Forgiveness,—love,—and winsome grace,
And for the penitent a place.

UNFADING GLORY

" Our light affliction, which is but for a moment, worketh for us a far more exceeding and eternal weight of glory ; while we look not at the things which are seen, but at the things which are not seen : for the things which are seen are temporal ; but the things which are not seen are eternal." II Cor. iv. 17-18.

" Eye hath not seen, nor ear heard, neither have entered into the heart of man, the things which God hath prepared for them that love Him." I Cor. ii. 9.

" Looking for that blessed hope, and the glorious appearing of the great God and our Saviour Jesus Christ." Tit. ii. 13.

" The city had no need of the sun, neither of the moon, to shine in it : for the glory of God did lighten it, and the Lamb is the light thereof. . . . There shall be no night there ; and they need no candle, neither light of the sun ; for the Lord God giveth them light : and they shall reign for ever and ever." Rev. xxi. 23, xxii. 5.

UNFADING glory ! That is what awaits us !
   Glory to pale not,—never to grow dim ;
  Glory to last throughout the countless ages
Of that new life which we shall share with Him.

Unfading glory ! Human comprehension
   Fails to conceive what that estate shall be :
Mind cannot know it, nor could words describe it—
   Glory eternal ; glory endlessly.

Meanwhile, perchance, affliction is life's portion,—
   Varied in form, nor welcomed as a guest :
Erringly deemed a burden or disaster,—
   That it might go—we reason would be best.

Stay ! Such affliction—lasting " for a moment ",
   Worketh a weight of glory yet to be :
Glory to last throughout the endless ages,—
   Unfading glory—through eternity.

LEST THEY FAINT IN THE WAY

" Jesus said, I have compassion on the multitude, because they continue with me now three days, and have nothing to eat : and I will not send them away fasting, lest they faint in the way." Mat. xv. 32.

" Jesus went forth, and saw a great multitude, and was moved with compassion toward them." Mat. xiv. 14.

" Like as a father pitieth his children, so the Lord pitieth them that fear Him. For He knoweth our frame ; He remembereth that we are dust." Psa. ciii. 13/14.

" When the morning was now come, Jesus stood on the shore . . . Children have ye any meat? They answered Him No . . . Jesus saith unto them, Come and dine." Jno. xxi. 4/13.

" LEST they faint in the way "—words of tender compassion !
    Not fasting—the Saviour would send them away :
They hungered ! He ordered, in sovereign-like fashion,
    A meal that would be both a strength and a stay.

" Lest they faint in the way ! " Is He not still as tender ?
    With pitying eye doth He not read our care ?
And will He forget sovereign help to us render,—
    Since all that concerns us He truly doth share ?

" Lest they faint in the way ! " Blessèd music to charm us
    When, jaded and way-worn, and drooping, we sink :
Our need He full knows,—dare we let it alarm us ?
    Will He not command for us food, yea, and drink ?

" Lest they faint in the way ! " Blessèd comfort in sorrow ;
    His grace He will send to support and sustain :
Thus, down through the years,—through each unknown tomorrow,
    " Lest they faint in the way " we can make our refrain.

STILL PRAISING THEE

"Blessed are they that dwell in Thy house : they will be still praising Thee." Psa. lxxxiv. 4.

"Whoso offereth praise glorifieth Me." Psa. l. 23.

"I will sing praises unto the Lord." Psa. xxvii. 6.

"Unto Him that loved us, and washed us from our sins in His own blood, and hath made us kings and priests unto God and His Father ; to Him be glory and dominion for ever and ever." Rev. i. 5-6.

"STILL praising Thee"! That should be my mission
    As fleeting years so quickly come and go :
"Still praising Thee",—be this my high ambition ;
    Then further cause for praising I shall know.

"Still praising Thee" for blessings freely given :
    "Still praising Thee" for mercies on life's way ;
"Still praising Thee" for all that comes from Heaven—
    Health, strength, and food—sufficient for each day.

"Still praising Thee" for that sublimest blessing—
    God's love, in Christ, so lavishly outpoured.
Oh, that these lips more ardent were confessing
    The wealth of bliss through Jesus Christ the Lord.

"Still praising Thee"! and looking for the Morning
    Soon, soon to break, when Christ shall come again :
Morn that shall burst, unheralded by warning,
    When He shall come, Whose right it is to reign.

THE SECRET OF REST

"We are troubled on every side, yet not distressed; we are perplexed, but not in despair." 2 Cor. iv. 8.

"We know that all things work together for good to them that love God." Rom. viii. 28.

"My peace I give unto you . . . Let not your heart be troubled." Jno. xiv. 27.

"There was given to me a thorn in the flesh . . . He said unto me, My Grace is sufficient for thee." 2 Cor. xii. 7/10.

THINGS oft go wrong! Our plans frustrated lie;
    And anxious care our peace-realm would molest:
With minds disturbed, we urgent question "Why?"
    And tend to lose our birthright—"Perfect Rest".

And friends, much trusted, seem to strangely fail;
    And, disappointed, we are apt to fret:
And brooding thoughts, unwanted, then assail,
    And we our source of victory forget.

And sorrows come, great, dark, and dire and deep;
    And mysteries engulf as doth the wave;
And somewhere, deep within, we know we weep,
    Although 'gainst all we would be strong and brave.

    *   *   *   *   *

To keep our peace we need an attitude;
    A sweet acceptance of this wondrous Word—
"We know all things are working for our good,
    For good alone, to them that love the Lord."

UNEXPECTED WAYS

" Blessed be the Lord God, the God of Israel, Who only doeth wondrous things." Psa. lxxii. 18.

" Marvellous things did He in the sight of their fathers, in the land of Egypt, in the field of Zoan. He divided the sea, and caused them to pass through ; and He made the waters to stand as an heap. In the daytime also He led them with a cloud, and all the night with a light of fire. He clave the rocks in the wilderness, and gave them drink as out of the great depths. He brought streams also out of the rock, and caused waters to run down like rivers." Psa. lxxviii. 12-16.

" They hired Balaam against them, that he should curse them : howbeit our God turned the curse into a blessing." Neh. xiii. 2.

'TIS good to dwell on years now past,
    And on those problem days
When we could only on Him cast
    The future with its maze :
To find He brought us through at last
    By unexpected ways.

'Tis good to view, yet once again,
    And grateful songs to raise,
On all that He did for us then,
    And to His name give praise :
He wrought for us, on things and men,
    By unexpected ways.

What if to-day we wistful stand,
    And on the future gaze ;
We see not far—nor understand—
    The road is wrapped in haze :
God still will lead, by His good hand,
    By unexpected ways.

GOD'S RIGHTEOUSNESS

"Blessed are they which do hunger and thirst after righteousness." Mat. v. 6.

"By the deeds of the law there shall no flesh be justified." Rom. iii. 20.

"They which receive . . . the gift of righteousness shall reign in life by one, Jesus Christ." Rom. v. 17.

"Christ is the end of the law for righteousness to everyone that believeth." Rom. x. 4.

"GOD's Righteousness!" Great word indeed!
   For Gentile sons, or Israel's seed;
     For every human soul of man!
God's Righteousness—is God's great plan.

What is "God's Righteousness" we ask.
To keep the law? Oh, futile task!
Who keeps the law in all detail?
The souls who try most truly fail.

"God's Righteousness" is none but Christ;
His life and death have quite sufficed:
The only "righteousness" there is
That pleases God, is surely His.

Ah, then, 'tis wise that we put on
The "righteousness" of God's dear Son:
Enough—when in Him thus we stand,
We have the "rightness" God hath planned.

UNSEARCHABLE RICHES

" Unto me, who am less than the least of all saints, is this grace given, that I should preach among the Gentiles the unsearchable riches of Christ." Eph. iii. 8.

" To whom God would make known what is the riches of the glory of this mystery among the Gentiles ; which is Christ in you, the hope of glory." Col. i. 27.

" Blessed be the God and Father of our Lord Jesus Christ, Who hath blessed us with all spiritual blessings in heavenly places in Christ. In Whom we have redemption through His blood, the forgiveness of sins, according to the riches of His grace." Eph. i. 3, 7.

" The fruit of the Spirit is love, joy, peace, longsuffering, gentleness, goodness, faith, meekness, temperance." Gal. v. 22-23.

UNSEARCHABLE riches,—unfailing, unending,
   Exhaustless and boundless—for thee and for me ;
Unsearchable wealth,—undiminished by spending,—
   Our riches in Christ—evermore ours to be.

His GRACE is unsearchable—vast beyond measure ;
   Always " sufficient "—in pressure or pain ;
Grace upon grace, oh, what wealth and what treasure;
   Grace that transforms direst loss into gain.

His PEACE is unsearchable—deep like a river ;
   Peace which prevails when the news might bring dread :
Peace which from panic doth surely deliver ;
   Yea, heart and mind keeping tranquil instead.

His JOY is unsearchable,—ever upspringing ;
   Dark days or bright days—no change it doth shew :
Sweetly sustaining, and strength daily bringing,—
   Joy—yes, unsearchable, and ours to know.

LED UNTO PILATE

"And the whole multitude of them arose and led Him (Jesus) unto Pilate." Lu. xxiii. 1.

"Then cried they all again, saying, Not this man, but Barabbas." Jno. xviii. 40.

"He is brought as a lamb to the slaughter, and as a sheep before her shearers is dumb, so He openeth not His mouth." Isa. liii. 7.

THEY led Him to Pilate—the multitude led Him,—
   The meek Son of God ; and He did not resist :
With unbridled passion they hustled and hounded,
   With fury and frenzy—they shrieked and they hissed.

They jeered and they jibed as their victim they jostled
   Through thoroughfares narrow to Pilate and death :
Not judgment they sought, 'twas His blood that they wanted ;
   Their lust for His blood filled their venomous breath.

"Barabbas" they shouted, "Release us Barabbas" ;
   A felon, a murderer,—such was their choice :
" Let this man be crucified ! Crucified ! Crucified ! "
   They shrieked out in madness, yea, all with one voice.

And Pilate delivered to hands yet more cruel
   The dear Son of God to be thus crucified :
Oh, ghastliest tragedy,—yet most blest wonder—
   The Saviour thus slain for mankind freely died.

UNSLEEPING WATCHFULNESS

"Behold, He that keepeth Israel shall neither slumber nor sleep." Psa. cxxi. 4.

"The eyes of the Lord run to and fro throughout the whole earth, to shew Himself strong in the behalf of them whose heart is perfect toward Him." II Chr. xvi. 9.

"If I say, Surely the darkness shall cover me ; even the night shall be light about me. Yea, the darkness hideth not from Thee ; but the night shineth as the day : the darkness and the light are both alike to Thee." Psa. cxxxix. 11-12.

"Are they (angels) not all ministering spirits, sent forth to minister for them who shall be heirs of salvation ?" Heb. i. 14.

HE slumbers not, nor sleeps,—the God Who thinks of thee,
Where'er thy life is placed, whate'er thy lot may be :
In sunshine or in shade, in comfort or distress,
His care surrounds thee with unsleeping watchfulness.

Our feeble minds forget He doth not weary grow :
He doth not ever tire, or fail all things to know :
And knowing—He doth care : and loving—He doth bless,
Bestowing night and day unsleeping watchfulness.

'Tis wondrous in our eyes ! We cannot comprehend
How He can hold all worlds and yet our lives attend :
Unworthy we may feel—He careth none the less,
Surrounding us, each one, with constant watchfulness.

Oh, give us minds to muse, and hearts to fitly praise,
And souls to worship Thee for all Thy wondrous ways:
Eternal life in Christ—the Christ our spirits bless,
And for our journey here—God's changeless watchfulness.

WHAT DID SHE WITH IT ?

"When Herod's birthday was kept, the daughter of Herodias danced before them, and pleased Herod. Whereupon he promised with an oath to give her whatsoever she would ask, and she, being before instructed of her mother, said, Give me here John Baptist's head in a charger." Mat. xiv. 6/8.

"And his head was brought in a charger, and given to the damsel: and she brought it to her mother." Mat. xiv. 11.

"And the Lord said unto Cain, Where is Abel thy brother. . . . The voice of thy brother's blood crieth unto Me from the ground." Gen. iv. 8/15.

"Against Thee, Thee only, have I sinned, and done this evil in Thy sight." Psa. li. 4.

WHAT did she with it—that noble head,
   Of him who was brave and strong ?
She fancied that if he were safely dead
   No voice would denounce her wrong.

What did she with it ? For there it lay !
   Full quick was the answer given :
Her paramour acted without delay,—
   While the angels wept in heaven.

What did she with it ? We cannot tell !
   Still deeper became sin's dye !
Still hotter became sin's awful hell !
   Still fiercer the conscience cry !

What did she with it ? It matters not !
   It matters that we, who read,
Should know that conscience, God's voice, could not
   Be stifled by such base deed.

One voice was stilled : it was faithful, true ;
   But there yelled through the cloisters grim
That sin was sin : and there joined it new
   A cry from the blood of him.

And the lesson—? Well, is it hard to learn ?
   Enchanting though sin may be,
It demands its toll, it is sure to burn,
   It produces its agony.

UNCHANGING BLESSINGS

" The eternal God is thy refuge, and underneath are the everlasting arms." Deut. xxxiii. 27.

" He knoweth the way that I take : when He hath tried me, I shall come forth as gold." Job xxiii. 10.

" The beloved of the Lord shall dwell in safety by Him ; and the Lord shall cover him all the day long, and he shall dwell between His shoulders." Deut. xxxiii. 12.

" He is our God ; and we are the people of His pasture, and the sheep of His hand." Psa. xcv. 7.

WE fain would write some word of warmest gladness—
    Some word of uplift, and of truest cheer ;
For—myriad are the things and themes of sadness,
    Which come to meet us with each passing year.

'Tis good to dwell on things which cannot perish,—
    Which cannot change, nor fade, nor yet decay ;
Those things which, deep within, we truly cherish,—
    And which can never, never pass away.

The Love of God,—all-reaching and availing !
    The Peace of God,—to keep both heart and mind !
The Power of God,—sufficient and unfailing !
    The Grace of God,—all wounds to soothe and bind !

The Presence here ; the glad and sweet communion !
    The wondrous welcome—waiting over There !
The Father's House,—and with those There what union !
    And endless joys, which cannot here compare.

JESUS OF NAZARETH

" The multitude said, This is Jesus the prophet of Nazareth."
Mat. xxi. 11.

" Is not this the carpenter, the son of Mary . . . ? " Mark vi. 3.

" When he (Bartimæus) heard that it was Jesus of Nazareth, he began to cry out. . ."   Mark x. 47.

" Be not affrighted : Ye seek Jesus of Nazareth which was crucified : He is risen."   Mark xvi. 1/6.

HE trod the lanes ; each street He knew ;
   Perchance each house He knew full well ;
   The country roads He traversed, too ;
Oft climbed each slope ; passed through each dell.

And there He toiled,—six days each week,—
   'Midst timber, saw-dust, shavings, glue ;
And peasant folk came oft to seek
   His skilful aid to help them through.

A chair ! A table ! Oft a yoke !
   A broken plough for Him to mend !
The constant needs of humble folk
   Came to the Carpenter,—their Friend.

And to their homes He oft would go,—
   And tools and timber carried there ;
Some wanted-thing—which they would show,
   Or to effect some small repair.

Oh, Nazareth ! Why honoured so ?
   How were ye blind to read His face ?
How were ye dull to Him not know,
   And deaf to hear His words of grace ?

And we, more honoured far than you,
   Should know Him in each passing day ;
His voice, His smile, His presence, too,
   Should be our portion in life's way.

NO VARIABLENESS

"Every good gift and every perfect gift is from above, and cometh down from the Father of lights, with Whom is no variableness, neither shadow of turning." Jas. i. 17.

"I am the Lord, I change not." Mal. iii. 6.

"They shall perish, but Thou remainest ; and they all shall wax old as doth a garment ; and as a vesture shalt Thou fold them up, and they shall be changed : but Thou art the same, and Thy years shall not fail." Heb. i. 11-12.

"Lord, Thou hast been our dwelling place in all generations. Before the mountains were brought forth, or ever Thou hadst formed the earth and the world, even from everlasting to everlasting, Thou art God." Psa. xc. 1-2.

NO variableness ! With whom ? Well, not with me ;
My heart is fixed ; and I would faithful be :
But yet, alas, I fail in constancy.

No variableness ! With whom ? Not e'en my friend,—
The dearest one,—on whom I might depend
Doth fail at times to rightly comprehend.

No variableness ! With whom ? With Him, my Lord !
It is the statement of His blessèd Word :
And they who know Him best with this accord.

Thus unto Him, when shadowed or distressed,
With all that would my inner soul molest,
I'll go for pardon, comfort, peace, and rest.

And shall I find that He is just the same,
E'en though, perchance, I have to come with shame ?
Ah, yes,—unchanged ! Thrice blessèd be His Name.

THEY MADE HIM A SUPPER.

" Jesus . . . came to Bethany. . . There they made Him a supper ; and Martha served."   Jno. xii. 1/9.

" Now Jesus loved Martha, and her sister, and Lazarus." Jno. xi. 5.

" Jesus answered them, Have not I chosen you twelve, and one of you is a devil? He spake of Judas Iscariot."   Jno. vi. 70/71.

"Blessed are they which are called unto the marriage supper of the Lamb."   Rev. xix. 9.

THEY made Him a supper ! He was to them dear !
   It was to be hallowed and rare ;
They wanted His presence unspeakably near,—
   But Judas, but Judas was there.

'Twas home unto Him, He Who no home possessed ;
   Oft there He found comfort and care :
This supper would be a sweet season of rest,—
   But Judas, but Judas was there.

The table was spread with the best that they had ;
   'Twould be the last supper He'd share :
They'd lavish their love, though their spirits were sad ;
   But Judas, but Judas was there.

The spikenard was poured,—it was love's willing price,—
   The sacred feet wiped with the hair ;
For Him, 'twas for Him,—thus not deemed sacrifice ;
   But Judas, but Judas was there.

Dark shade on the love-feast ! Base wreckage of joy !
   Pretence for the poor to have care !
Love's purest devotion to vilely destroy !
   Base Judas,—base Judas was there.

They made *Him* a supper ! He yet will give one
   'Gainst which there is none can compare ;
'Twill be at the Marriage of God's beloved Son,—
   And I, wondrous fact, shall be there !

No shadow shall fall on that wonderful feast,
   Set yonder in heaven so fair :
No cloud will oppress,—and no sin, not the least,—
   No Judas nor sin will be There.

THINGS PRESENT

"I am persuaded that neither death, nor life, nor angels, nor principalities, nor powers, nor things present, nor things to come, nor height, nor depth, nor any other creature, shall be able to separate us from the love of God, which is in Christ Jesus our Lord." Rom. viii. 38-39.

"Lest I should be exalted . . . there was given to me a thorn in the flesh. . . . For this thing I besought the Lord thrice, that it might depart from me. And He said unto me, My grace is sufficient for thee." II Cor. xii. 7-9.

"There hath no temptation taken you but such as is common to man : but God is faithful, Who will not suffer you to be tempted above that ye are able ; but will with the temptation also make a way to escape, that ye may be able to bear it." 1 Cor. x. 13.

"In weariness and painfulness, in watchings often, in hunger and thirst, in fastings often, in cold and nakedness. Beside those things . . . the care of all the churches." II Cor. xi. 27-28.

THEY tend to upset us—the things which are present,—
   The burdens, the cares, and the claims of to-day,—
The things which to us seem so very unpleasant,
   We wish, oh so much, they would not come our way.

We deem them unwelcome, those trying "things present" ;
   Could we but arrange it they ne'er would come near!
But come—? why, they do,—constant, ceaseless, incessant ;
   From sources undreamt-of they sudden appear.

Well, were we without them we would be much poorer;
   If paths were all rosy we might deem it best :
Yet, sooner or later, there is nothing surer,
   Set free from all trials would find us less blest.

If present things try us His grace is sufficient ;
   If burdens oppress we may make Him our stay :
If our own resources we find are deficient
   'Twill drive us to Him Whose strength ne'er can give way.

MY PEACE I LEAVE WITH YOU

"Peace I leave with you, My peace I give unto you. . . Let not your heart be troubled." Jno. xiv. 27.

"The peace of God, which passeth all understanding, shall keep your hearts and minds through Christ Jesus." Phil. iv. 7.

"Thou wilt keep him in perfect peace, whose mind is stayed on Thee." Isa. xxvi. 3.

GREAT legacy He left His own—
'Twas left to them, to them alone,—
The peace which He Himself had known.

This peace would keep us every day,—
'Midst all the world's distracted fray ;
We may possess it now—alway.

No effort brings it to our door ;
Nor need we for its wealth implore ;
'Tis ours : exhaustless in its store.

How comes it ? Well—" My peace I leave ; "
'Tis ours as we His Word believe ;
It keeps—as we its wealth receive.

PERPLEXED
(But not in despair)

"We are troubled on every side, yet not distressed; we are perplexed, but not in despair." II Cor. iv. 8.

"Why art thou cast down, O my soul? and why art thou disquieted in me? Hope thou in God: for I shall yet praise Him for the help of His countenance." Psa. xlii. 5.

"I was envious at the foolish, when I saw the prosperity of the wicked. . . . They are not in trouble as other men; neither are they plagued like other men. . . . Behold, these are the ungodly, who prosper in the world; they increase in riches. Verily I have cleansed my heart in vain, and washed my hands in innocency. . . . When I thought to know this, it was too painful for me, until I went into the sanctuary of God; then understood I their end." Psa. lxxiii. 3, 5, 12, 13, 16, 17.

PERPLEXED? Oh, yes,—the answer is not given;
   The dark enigmas press upon the soul:
We cry,—but, lo, no answer comes from Heaven;
   And deep and dark the billows o'er us roll.

Perplexed? Oh, yes, the "why" of things sore presses;
   It will not stay, nor stifle, nor be still;
It fain would drive us to uncertain guesses
   About the meaning of God's sovereign will.

Why He permits so much that seems appalling;
   Why He withholds His sovereign hand and power;
"Why, why, oh, why," from thousand hearts is calling
   In what, e'en now, is earth's still darkening hour.

Perplexed? Oh, yes, but truly not despairing;
   Our God—omnipotent, supreme reigns still:
He for His own is truly hourly caring;
   And for His world is working out His will.

FEAR AND FAMINE

"There shall be signs in the sun, and in the moon, and in the stars ; and upon the earth distress of nations, with perplexity ; . . . men's hearts failing them for fear, and for looking after those things which are coming on the earth : for the powers of heaven shall be shaken." Lu. xxi. 25, 26.

"There is no fear in love ; but perfect love casteth out fear : because fear hath torment." 1 Jno. iv. 18.

"We should be saved from our enemies, and from the hand of all that hate us . . . that we being delivered out of the hand of our enemies might serve Him without fear." Lu. 1. 68/79.

WIDESPREAD famine doth appear !
Stricken souls are gripped with fear !
Woes now growing o'er the earth ;
Ills which leave no room for mirth ;
Fear which fills men's hearts with dread ;
Famine claiming countless dead.

Whither shall we fly for rest
In these days so much distressed ?
Whither shall we turn for peace ?
How shall mental anguish cease ?
How— ? By, in these evil days,
Making Him our hope always.

Will He fail us ? Surely nay !
He shall be our strength and stay !
Mind and heart when on Him stayed
Know not fear—are not afraid :
And whate'er our needs may be,
He can meet them wondrously.

BAD NEWS—BUT GOD !

" We were pressed out of measure, above strength, insomuch that we despaired even of life : but we had the sentence of death in ourselves, that we should not trust in ourselves, but in God which raiseth the dead : Who delivered us from so great a death, and doth deliver : in Whom we trust that He will yet deliver us." II Cor i. 8-10.

" Now if ye be ready, that at what time ye hear . . . all kinds of music, ye fall down and worship the image which I have made ; well : but if ye worship not, ye shall be cast the same hour into the midst of a burning fiery furnace ; and who is that God that shall deliver you out of my hands ? . . . O Nebuchadnezzar, we are not careful to answer thee in this matter. If it be so, our God, Whom we serve, is able to deliver us from the burning fiery furnace, and He will deliver us out of thine hand, O king." Dan. iii. 15-17.

BAD news has come, and heart and mind are sobered,—
    We did not think that things would come to this ;
We deemed that God would surely send deliverance ;
    We asked that what was threatened we might miss.

But it has come—the thing we deemed unwanted !
    Bad news, indeed, it seems to us to-day ;
We cannot think that God has failed to hear us,
    But cannot fathom why He answers " Nay ".

What shall we do ? Succumb or get downhearted ?
    That were, indeed, the easy road to tread ;
With hope and trust cast over,—faith abandoned,—
    And God—the God Who loves—why, deemed as dead.

Bad news indeed ! But God abideth faithful !
    Some fresh unfolding of His power He'll shew ;
Thus, unto Him, Whose love is quite unending,
    Whose care and power are limitless,—we'll go.

MY TIMES AND GOD'S HAND

"My times are in Thy hand." Psa. xxxi. 15.

"He performeth the thing that is appointed for me." Job. xxiii. 14.

"Ye ought to say, if the Lord will, we shall live, and do this, or that." James iv. 15.

"In Him we live, and move, and have our being." Acts xvii. 28.

My times are in Thy hand !
   Not mine to know the years !
Then should I apprehensive be
   Or harbour needless fears ?

My times are in Thy hand :
   Thou hast Thy plan for me ;
And, if surrendered I remain,
   Thy plan fulfilled shall be.

My times are in *Thy* hand !
   This, then, should be my rest :
My tale of years I cannot say,
   How should that be my quest ?

Enough—that I am Thine,
   And have Thy work to do :
And Thou Who givest me my task
   Wilt surely see me through.

UNENDING GOODNESS

" Thou shalt remember all the way which the Lord thy God led thee."   Deut. viii. 2.

" He is our God ; and we are the people of His pasture, and the sheep of His hand."   Psa. xcv. 7.

" Thou shalt guide me with Thy counsel, and afterward receive me to glory."   Psa. lxxiii. 24.

" The Lord is thy keeper : the Lord is thy shade upon thy right hand. . . . The Lord shall preserve thy going out and thy coming in from this time forth, and even for evermore."   Psa. cxxi. 5, 8.

THESE simple thoughts perhaps are worth repeating,
    They may give strength on life's eventful road ;
Years come and go, and Time keeps onward fleeting ;
    How good to have the soul stayed calm in God.

How good to muse,—in happy, sweet reflection,—
    O'er all the way by which His hand hath led !
How strengthening and rich the recollection
    Of all His goodness in the years now fled.

How wise to pause,—to make the courage stronger,—
    And stay the soul more surely on His Word,—
For days to come,—for years,—life may be longer ;
    To make the spirit's anchorage—The LORD.

He will not fail !   His Word cannot be broken.
    He gave His Best !—shall He not all else give ?
No need to ask for sign, or sense, or token,—
    But just to trust His Word, and with Him live.

ORDERED STEPS

"The steps of a good man are ordered by the Lord." Psa. xxxvii. 23.

"Thou shalt guide me with Thy counsel, and afterward receive me to glory." Psa. lxxiii. 24.

"In all thy ways acknowledge Him, and He shall direct thy paths." Pro. iii. 6.

WHAT comfort 'tis this truth to know—
If we please Him while here below
Our daily steps He will direct,
Which means He surely will protect.

No need to agonizing pray
That He will guide us on life's way:
He's said He'll do it,—we may rest,
And find He leads in paths most blest.

Our " steps " He speaks of,—not our flight,—
Our daily steps He'll guide aright;
He *has been* guiding till this day;
Why should we fear He'll let us stray?

Years come and go, with loss and change;
The path is oft-times new and strange:
But His strong hand, unerring skill,
And perfect knowledge, order still.

Yes, there we rest! 'Tis His sure Word;
Our steps are ordered by the Lord;
And this would be our happy sense—
That we in Him have confidence.

THANKSGIVING

" Enter into His gates with thanksgiving, and into His courts with praise: be thankful unto Him, and bless His name." Psa. c. 4.

" Be ye thankful." Col. iii. 15.

" In every thing give thanks: for this is the will of God in Christ Jesus concerning you." I Thes. v. 18.

" Be careful for nothing: but in every thing by prayer and supplication, with thanksgiving, let your requests be made known unto God." Phil. iv. 6.

WE thank Thee, Lord, for peaceful days,
   When cannon's roar throbs not the breast;
For peace to go our lawful ways,
   No more by hideous war distressed.

For quiet nights—for sleep thus given—
   Unrent by sounds that terrify;
No screaming shells crash now from heaven,
   Nor cruel bombers fill our sky.

We thank Thee for this respite given!
   We pray that men may turn to Thee—
May think of God, and Christ, and Heaven,
   And of the vast Eternity.

And for ourselves, so richly blest,
   Redeemed by Christ—through Him forgiven—
His life by us should be confessed
   As daily we draw nearer Heaven.

CAN GOD ? OR GOD CAN !

"They spake against God; they said, Can God furnish a table in the wilderness?" Psa. lxxviii. 19.

"Sirs, be of good cheer; for I believe God, that it shall be even as it was told me." Acts xxvii. 25.

"Our God Whom we serve is able to deliver us." Dan. iii. 17.

"Now unto Him that is able to do exceeding abundantly above all that we ask or think . . . unto Him be glory." Eph. iii. 20/21.

"CAN God," they said, "Can He provide?"
Their evil hearts did Him deride :
How came they to forget the past ;
The highway through the waters cast ;
The cloudy pillar—night and day ;
The rocks He clave their thirst to stay ;
The Manna,—angels' food,—from heaven ;
Meat to the full, and daily given ?

"Can God ? " Oh, hearts of unbelief !
When He so oft had sent relief ;
Had shewn such wonders in the way ;
No law, no power His might could stay :
No need could rise He could not meet :
No obstacle His will defeat ;
For He was God,—and their God, too ;
And yet they sneered—" Can God this do ? "

Shall we reverse those words to-day ?
Shall we "God can !"—all fearless say ?
Whate'er our lot, our case, our need,
Perplexing though it be, indeed,—
Shall we make this our heart's refrain,—
" God can ! God can ! " Then not in vain
Shall we Him honour : faith shall see
God works for such trust wondrously.

UNFAILING MERCIES

"In Him we live, and move, and have our being." Acts xvii. 28.

"Bless the Lord, O my soul, and forget not all His benefits: Who forgiveth all thine iniquities; Who healeth all thy diseases; Who redeemeth thy life from destruction; Who crowneth thee with lovingkindness and tender mercies; Who satisfieth thy mouth with good things; so that thy youth is renewed like the eagle's." Psa. ciii. 2-5.

"Like as a father pitieth his children, so the Lord pitieth them that fear Him. For He knoweth our frame; He remembereth that we are dust." Psa. ciii. 13-14.

THIS little message would have for its mission
To greet each reader on life's stretching road;
And this would also be its true ambition—
To strengthen, even more, their hand in God.

God never changes! Things and people alter;
And blessings, one time prized, with time grow dim;
He changes not,—nor varies,—nor doth falter;
And we are ever rich in having Him.

God's love abides,—though other loves may perish;
Though streams, whereat we drank, may sadly dry:
Yea,—though some love may fail we much did cherish,
We still may find in Him a sure supply.

And—to God's care there surely is no ending!
He who gave Christ can not withhold His care:
And we may know the joy of His attending,—
And in the hour of need shall find Him there!